TAKE CHARGE
OF YOUR CHILD'S
EDUCATION!

TAKE CHARGE OF YOUR CHILD'S EDUCATION!

How Parents are Taking an
INDIVIDUALIZED MAVERICK APPROACH
to Homeschool Their Children to Success

MARY RESENBECK

Unstoppable CEO Press

Mary Resenbeck
resenbeckm@yahoo.com
recas-resenbeckseducationalconsulting.com

Take Charge of Your Child's Education! Mary Resenbeck —1st ed.
ISBN 978-1-955242-09-7

CONTENTS

Dedication

I dedicate this book to my husband, Doug, my rock, and my best friend. Also, to my three children, Douglas, Alexis, and Grace. They are my light, love, and treasures. I also dedicate this book to my mom for always loving and supporting me. I am lucky to have loving family and friends by my side. God has blessed me. Thank you all so very much. Love you forever.

Epigraph

"Do not go where the path may lead. Go instead where there is no path and leave a trail."

– Ralph Waldo Emerson

Introduction

Welcome to the wonderful world of homeschooling.

In a few years, you will look back on your experience and you will see that it will have been one of your crowning achievements as a parent.

You'll have given your child a leg up on most other students that come out of the public—or even private—school system.

Busting the Myths

Many people will direct certain statements at you to steer you clear from your choice to homeschool your child, but in reality, they are all myths. Well-meaning friends and family will tell you parents aren't capable of teaching academic subjects correctly, colleges don't accept homeschoolers, or homeschooled children don't know how to socialize with their peers. Another misconception about homeschooling is that their parents can't adequately homeschool children with special needs. These statements are all incorrect.

During COVID-19, the world suddenly shifted to families homeschooling their children, and the school districts couldn't handle the sudden change because they weren't equipped. They did not understand how to guide children's education from home appropriately. The burden of education was on the parents, and teachers were left to swim in the unknown abyss of online learning, which frustrated many.

Parents' role was often to make sure that the kids attended their online classes, that the computer equipment was working, and keep the kids motivated, which seemed impossible for many families. Their children were unhappy with the lack of connection, hands-on learning, and meaningful interaction. Some will argue that the pandemic was to blame, and educators will say learning from home is too hard, but the truth was the lack of purposeful organic homeschool direction.

If you picked up this book, it's because you are considering home-schooling for your kids.

It may be because your child has what schools call a "learning disability" or simply because you are **unhappy** with the school system.

I understand—I've been there.

Welcome to the world of The Resenbeck Maverick Homeschool Methods!

When I talk about "maverick", I mean nontraditional, unconventional, unorthodox, and independent academic methods.

Think of Tom Cruise in Top Gun. He didn't follow the rules and did it his way. That's why he was nicknamed "Maverick".

And if you're considering homeschooling, then you are a maverick too. You are free to educate your children *your* way. After all, it is *your* child...

Plus, you're in great company!

A Legion of Millions

In 2021, the US Census Bureau (USCB) conducted a survey to determine how American families were managing the COVID-19 pandemic. The original intent of the survey was to determine whether family members still had jobs or were eating sufficiently and how children were faring in school.

That survey showed that the decision to homeschool had gone up dramatically.

According to the survey, 3.2 million parents were homeschooling their kids at the beginning of 2020. In 2021, that number had jumped to over 5 million.

That number represents families, but according to the National Center for Educational Statistics (NCES), 75% of homeschooling families have more than one child.

They estimate that at least 8 million children are now being home-schooled.

That's quite a community, and it keeps growing. In fact, in 2015 the NCES estimated that there were only about 5.8 million students in private schools.

You are not alone in considering homeschooling.

GROWTH OF HOMESCHOOLING IN THE UNITED STATES

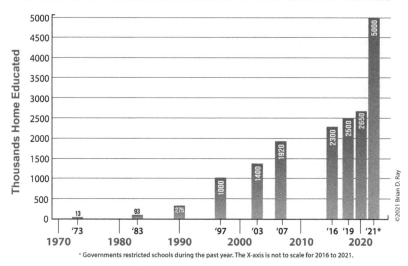

* Governments restricted schools during the past year. The X-axis is not to scale for 2016 to 2021.

www.nheri.org/research-facts-on-homeschooling/

Why I Wrote This Book

Many parents feel lost when it's time to start homeschooling.

They feel unsure of themselves because they don't have a blueprint for it, and they feel like they won't know how to teach their kids.

Many parents feel like homeschooling is the right answer for their child, but they don't know where to start.

I wrote this book to give you a roadmap to successfully homeschool your child efficiently and effortlessly with stress-free methods. My goal is to help you create a plan to make homeschooling effective and fun for you, your child, and your entire family.

Your kids will have a better educational experience, and you'll be able to homeschool without it consuming all your time.

You will not have to become a full-time educator, and you won't feel like you're flying blind.

Too many would-be homeschool parents give up before they even start because they surrender to homeschooling myths and don't embrace the freedom, independence, and different methodologies homeschooling offers. Unfortunately, many children get lost in public schools not designed for them; they lack the one-on-one attention they need. Therefore, homeschooling would be an appropriate choice for them and their family.

What happened during COVID-19 is not what homeschooling is supposed to represent. COVID-19 was crisis homeschooling.

Parents did not decide what to teach their kids, nor were they able to decide how to teach them.

Parents were at the mercy of whatever resources that their school and district made available to them.

That's **_not_** homeschooling. ***That's crisis management***.

Homeschooling, done right, is a pleasurable and rewarding experience.

My goal is for you to see that homeschooling is a valid way to learn and something that your whole family will appreciate and take to heart.

By the end of this book, you will be ready to embark on this extraordinary lifelong Homeschooling path of Maverick Learning which gives parents the ability to take charge of their child's education skillfully.

SECTION 1

Homeschooling Advantages

The Homeschooler's Advantage

Many advantages come with homeschooling, and the benefits might surprise you. Privately, homeschooling frees you to choose the right curriculum for your child's individualized learning style and provides:

- Personalized educational attention,
- Liberation of your child's mind,
- A stress-free, self-directed, enthusiastic learning environment.

Homeschooling gives parents the freedom to implement and deliver specific academic attention for children with invisible learning differences. Homeschooling enables children who have ADHD, dyslexia, dysgraphia, dyscalculia, or are 2e (twice-exceptional) or are on the Asperger Spectrum, etc., to flourish and shine when using a personalized homeschool philosophy. Gifted and 2e children are motivated to explore their interests, talents, and gifts and often progress faster than in a public-school setting.

A demographically wide variety of people homeschool—these are atheists, Christians, and Mormons; conservatives, libertarians, and liberals; low-, middle-, and high-income families; Black, Hispanic, and white; parents with PhDs, GEDs, and no high-school diplomas. One nationwide study shows that 41% of homeschool students are Black, Asian, Hispanic, and others (i.e., not White/non-Hispanic).[1]

Homeschooling accommodates all cultures, religions, secular families, and academic levels. It inspires different volunteering opportunities and entrepreneurship action because there are more ways to include those passions into the individualized schedule of the day, contributing to the family unit and the community in a positive way.

That said, it is important to know the different options available through homeschooling. You will need to research different homeschooling philosophies, what each method entails, and how to do it victoriously. This book will address some of that and will reduce the amount of research you need to do.

Successful homeschooling requires knowledge. Here are some to consider:

- **Local laws**: What homeschooling laws are applicable in your state? While homeschooling is legal everywhere in the United States, how you are allowed to do it varies from one state to another.

- **Resources**: As homeschooling gains in popularity, you have more resources at your disposal. Which resources are available to you locally, what do they offer, and what are the costs?

---

[1] U.S. Department of Education, 2019

- **Learning styles**: Each child has a learning style that allows them to succeed and thrive. By understanding and recognizing your child's unique learning style, you can adapt your homeschooling methods to best fit their needs.

- **Teaching methods**: There are many teaching methods in the homeschooling realm. Which ones are best suited to your child's learning style, your homeschooling approach, and your available time and resources?

One of the main reasons that parents take their children out of the traditional school system is because traditional methods don't work for their kids. This can be because the system itself is flawed or because their children need special care that the school can't—or won't—provide.

But if you're going to be successful at homeschooling, you need to address all the failings of the school system that didn't work for your child, which can be done well with the right plan of action and by utilizing the resources available.

Knowing the Laws

Here are some things to know about homeschool laws across the United States:

- It's legal to homeschool in all 50 states.
- Homeschooling laws vary in each state.
- Some states have a record-keeping requirement to ensure that there is proof learning is happening.
- This record-keeping includes attendance and may require a curriculum evidence binder.

Every state has their own requirements, and some have more than others.

Understanding the laws in your state helps you when you're moving from one state to another. Just because you could do something in one state doesn't mean the homeschooling laws are the same in another state.

Homeschooling Should Never Be Overwhelming

Many parents give up on the homeschooling idea because they *think* there is so much work involved.

If you decide to privately homeschool, understand you will not get a lot of support from the school system. At times, you may feel like you are on your own, but it doesn't need to be that way if you are aware of your educational rights.

The school system may not like that you choose homeschooling because each student that leaves public school means less funding for that district.

Taxpayers spend an average of $15,240 per pupil annually in public schools, plus capital expenditures. Today's roughly 4.5 million homeschool students represent a savings of over $68 billion for taxpayers. This is $68 billion that American taxpayers do not have to spend.[2]

---

[2] National Education Association, 2021, www.nheri.org/research-facts-on-homeschooling/

So, if you request help, the district may be hesitant, but there are requirements they are obligated to provide depending on your circumstances. I've dealt with many school districts that didn't know what homeschooling looks like, what parents were allowed or not allowed to do, or what their duties are toward parents.

Please understand and realize legally you ***do not*** have to be a professional educator to homeschool your child successfully. There are various ways to homeschool, and many credentialed teachers cross over to private homeschooling. They are available to help fill in the academic gaps if parents feel unsure about teaching certain core subjects.

Starting out, you may wonder what type of schooling approach to use and which method is the best suited for your child?

How do you build a plan with a varying curriculum, so you foster independent learning, and your child is encouraged to explore, investigate, master core subjects, and important life skills?

This requires a diverse, personalized curriculum, so you don't do the same things every single day.

And of course, you need to monitor the progress of your child, to make sure that the methods and the approaches you use are having the effect you want. There are ways to know that you are meeting all the milestones for your child to have a complete education.

Managing Homeschooling and Other Responsibilities

When you homeschool, you still must maintain your home, do the groceries, the laundry, the house chores, and so on.

Before homeschooling, you had a clear separation between school and home. The kids went to school every day at the same time and came back every afternoon at the same time. School was a physically different environment.

All of that disappears with homeschooling. It's all mixed in together. The only limits are the ones that you decide to put in place.

Turning everyday moments into academic and life skill learning experiences effortlessly is my expertise.

Homeschooling and Maintaining Your Job

Some homeschooling parents can change their schedule to allow them time to teach and work. But what do you do if you can't change your schedule, and quitting your job is not an option?

Never Give Up

Yes, there are many aspects to consider once you decide to home-school. No matter what, in the end, it will be worth it.

Even though it may seem overwhelming at times, I can assure you that it is feasible.

Many of my clients have been able to homeschool their kids successfully while keeping their job and all their existing responsibilities.

And my goal is to do the same for you.

The Right Homeschooling Approach for You

One of the early decisions you will make in your homeschooling journey is the type of homeschooling you want to do.

There are different types of homeschooling models, and each has their pros and cons.

The one that is best suited to your family will depend on your situation.

In this chapter, I briefly explain some of the homeschooling options in California (there are variations in every state) and who they are best suited for.

Method 1: District K-12 Online Homeschooling

Many families like the district public school style of K-12 online schooling; an example is Connections Academy. The online district homeschool programs provide families with state-certified educators to teach core subjects online and implement a ready-made state-approved curriculum as well as online parent support. This option works well for working students like actors, professional children athletes, or families looking solely for a free, complete accredited online opportunity.

District Charter Homeschool Options

A charter homeschool goes through your local school district. Still, unlike the K-12 online options, parents have more independence in delivering different state-approved curriculums. Families receive educational state funding for school supplies, books, academic enrichment programs, and extracurricular activities. The district provides each family an HST (Home School Teacher) to oversee the parents' teaching methods and track and test the student's progress monthly.

Recently, in California, the school unions have been pushing to end public funding for charter homeschool options because the state resources leave neighborhood brick and mortar schools and there are complaints about the lack of oversight on where the money goes. New rules and regulations are now in place to stifle families' academic decisions and interrupt their right to educate their children in a flexible, personalized way.

District homeschool charter schools can be a positive thing if your child has an IEP and you feel comfortable that they will adhere to the legal requirements of your child's IEP needs.

I have found, though, that sometimes the kids fall through the cracks.

Some kids with IEPs have been left behind, especially with parents who don't quite know the laws that navigate the IEP process.

The district charter homeschool method may be best if:

- Your child has an IEP, and the district cooperates fully with your teaching approach and provides appropriate services and accommodations needed for the child to academically thrive and succeed.
- You want a flexible learning schedule for your family but also want to utilize regionally accredited teachers, free resources, and a state-approved curriculum.
- Your family needs the extra funding the state provides to get the necessary enrichment classes needed to foster talents your family would otherwise never afford to provide for your child like horseback riding, tennis, or dance, etc.

I find most homeschool district programs take a heavy-handed approach to dealing with homeschool parents. Often, they restrict independence and oversee daily schedules and curriculum. I don't recommend these choices to families looking for a stress-free educational alternative and want to choose flexibility and seek freedom to select the style and method to teach their children.

Method 2: Private School Affidavit and Umbrella Programs (PSS)

When I decided to homeschool my two teenage kids, I opted for a private school affidavit. (PSA). This is specific to California, but other states have similar requirements.

With the PSA, you register your home as a school and identify yourself as the teacher and administrator. At that point, your home is considered a private school. We later joined an 'umbrella school'—another term is private satellite school.

You pick the curriculum, determine how it's administered, and choose the learning style. There is no district interference.

In other words, the district is not checking on the curriculum and not testing the kids. That removes a lot of the pressure from your kids—and from your entire family.

I chose this approach for my 2e (twice-exceptional) kids because it addressed my children's severe dyslexia, dysgraphia, and dyscalculia during their high school years. It immediately alleviated the daily stress from teachers refusing to adhere to their IEPs, implementing unnecessary testing, and overloading them with homework. It was affecting their mental health negatively. Once we began private homeschooling, I immediately saw an improvement academically and emotionally. My children both successfully graduated high school and were accepted into their college of choice. It was the best decision for our family, and that was when I began consulting other families wanting to take the private homeschooling approach. It hands families the power to do what they deem necessary to make their kids healthy and make their learning productive. After all, they are *your* children, and you know what is best for them.

This method is best if:

- You plan on doing the teaching yourself.
- You have a vibrant network of other homeschooling parents in your area, so you can share teaching duties and schedule social gatherings.
- You want to plan and execute a curriculum throughout the year.

Choosing to Join a Private Satellite School (Umbrella Program)

These private homeschools file the PSA for you, but it's filed under their school's name. Your home becomes a smaller "campus" of a larger private homeschool.

Once again, there is no district involvement. Families have complete freedom to choose a personalized way to educate their children. The umbrella school gives parents the opportunity to determine the best curriculum to use since the parents are the teachers.

The advantage of a PSA or a private umbrella (PSS) school is you have access to academic enrichment classes and family co-op programs, which are activities done in cooperation with the private homeschool and neighborhood homeschooling families. For example, my seven-year-old daughter attends a center which hosts academic enrichment classes two days a week. As a result, she has creative classes with other kids, goes on field trips, takes lunch breaks with friends, and has recess with them. That helps with her socialization skills and gives the family a sense of support and community.

My daughter also takes dance classes and has access to all the private extracurricular activities offered through the homeschool community. During the week, you can sign your child up for academic and enrichment classes hosted in a local park, a neighborhood home, a church campus, etc., and they may offer drop-off days where you drop your kids off like a traditional school. In that case, other teachers (some credentialed, some not, depending on what you are looking for and your family's preference) do the schooling during the hours the children are learning at an academic enrichment center.

This method is best if:

- You want your child to socialize with other children, but you don't want them to be on a campus every day.
- You want your child to have experienced educators teaching topics that you can't teach (for example, algebra, chemistry, dancing, or soccer).

This is my favorite form of homeschooling for families because of the freedom of choice in all aspects of the education they can create for their child. Families can travel, experience life adventures together, and children can concentrate on their interests without the district dictating how, what, and when your children learn.

Unschooling—A Unique Style of Curriculum

Unschooling is an educational approach growing in popularity among parents who prefer a different school atmosphere for their kids. Unschooling was the curriculum pedagogy I chose for my teenage children during their high school years, and it was the best move. As 2e individuals, this method allowed them to focus on their talents, gifts, passions, and interests, which bolstered their self-confidence even after college. Unschooling offers a way of learning that doesn't rely on classroom teaching or textbooks. Instead, it allows children to learn from experience through plenty of play and creative activities like house chores, looking after family pets, and even working part-time to gain valuable money skills.

Children are encouraged to explore everything that piques their curiosity while still being given guidance and affirmation by the parents.

In unschooling, homework is replaced with projects like growing vegetables or writing an eBook. It has its roots in a philosophy that advocates creating well-rounded individuals through experiential learning, generally by pursuing the activities and hobbies they are passionate about.

Unschoolers believe that you never stop learning and encourage children to take intellectual risks and to celebrate what they learn rather than just remember it.

This method is best if:

- You want your child to become an "out of the box" thinker.
- You believe that your child has enough natural curiosity and maturity to motivate himself or herself.
- You can provide the resources and opportunities that match your child's interests as they evolve.

World Schooling Methodology and Philosophy

World Schooling is the practice of homeschooling away from home by traveling and gaining first-hand experience with the whole family. This method exposes children to different cultures and lifestyles which in turn help them learn more about the world.

We were able to begin our youngest daughter's homeschooling this way. She traveled with us to several different states in the USA, visiting NASA in Houston, Texas, the Gateway Arch in Missouri,

New York City, and we took her to see the Statue of Liberty. When we traveled to Europe, she went to Ireland, England, and France. Many sights, sounds, experiences, foods, cultures, religions, customs, and languages were a whirlwind of experiential learning that she will never forget. It is seared into her memory and attached to family bonding as well. World schooling, of course, is a beautiful way to teach your child, registering with a PSS, and matching an Unschooling philosophy with World Schooling was a natural choice at the time for our family.

Your family does not need to be wealthy to create a world school environment, but it requires a lot of research and planning to be efficient and stress-free. This type of homeschooling is not for everyone, but it has been proven to be unique and beneficial to the learning experience for the entire family.

PROS OF
WORLDSCHOOLING,
AS TOLD BY THE KIDS

WITNESSING CULTURES FIRST HAND

The ability to learn from real world experiences rather than textbooks and technology is valued. Seeing, doing and immersing oneself in a country's language, history, infrastructure and natural environment are viewed as key to learning.

MEETING NEW PEOPLE

Making new friends, learning from locals and seeing the world through a different set of eyes is enjoyed and embraced. Difference and diversity is no barrier for these kids!

THE FOOD!

Discovering new flavours and cuisines is just one of the many joys of travelling, and it's not lost on even the youngest of these travellers!

SPENDING TIME WITH PARENTS

Time spent as a family is appreciated and awaited with anticipation. Parents are viewed simultaneously as educational guides and as a source of fun.

FLEXIBILITY OF LEARNING

Having a say in how, where, when, and what they learn is empowering and motivating for these kids. Individual preferences can be considered and styles of learning can be adapted to suit current needs.

Source
Little Green Globetrotter, www.littlegreenglobetrotter.com

Many world schooling academic approaches occur online, so your child has the freedom to learn anywhere, anytime. It provides a unique educational approach that combines world schooling with the best of online education and hands-on interactive learning with the surrounding communities.

This method is best if:

- You frequently travel for work, and you don't want to spend time away from your kids.
- You want your kids to experience life outside of the classroom.
- You want to expose your kids to many different cultures and customs, so they can have a well-rounded view of the world.

How I Discovered the Secret of Education Success While Teaching in the Classroom

When I married in 1995, my husband told me he was dyslexic, but I didn't know what that was. I didn't think much of it until we lived together as a married couple.

When I saw how he wrote a grocery list, I thought he was playing a joke on me, but I realized his dyslexia and dysgraphia were severe. Then, I noticed the same things with our children.

My Son's Story

My son is brilliant. He would talk politics at three, but he couldn't understand or recognize a letter. He has Asperger's and has some sensory problems as well.

At the time, I didn't know what Asperger's was because it wasn't understood well enough yet. When I heard autism, I only thought of the most severe forms. I didn't realize that there was a spectrum.

I was terrified as a young mother because my son felt like an anomaly. I was scared to send him to public school.

I remembered what I went through in school as a child. Teachers didn't take me seriously and chalked me up to being too social and lazy academically. In reality, it was because I couldn't pay attention. I would probably be considered ADHD by today's standards.

I couldn't imagine what kind of ridicule my son would face.

I decided to send Douglas to a wonderful private performing arts school in our neighborhood because he liked theater so much. I figured if he could hone his talents in a performing arts school, we would figure out the rest.

It was a great fit for him because of the creative aspect, but the first two years academically were difficult because I kept getting reports saying that he was bright, articulate, and opinionated. He showed promise in math, but he couldn't read or write at all.

I wanted to help, but because I wasn't at the school, I wasn't sure how to do that. They had an opening for a drama teacher, so I applied. The director accepted me because of my ample theater background and my acting and stage experience.

My son's classroom was directly across from the class where I worked as a teacher's assistant, and one day, I heard my son's teacher raise her voice and say loudly, "You're not listening!" It echoed throughout the halls.

I didn't need to be inside the classroom to know who she was speaking to; it was directed toward my son. My stomach just dropped to my toes, and I thought, "How am I going to handle this?"

I understood her frustration because it was my frustration. This educator was a seasoned and beloved teacher with many years of experience. I respected her, and I believed if we could work as a team, my son would benefit, and so would I.

At the break, I went to see her, and I explained that I responded to Douglas the same way when my patience had worn out during reading and writing at home. I knew the encounter I heard throughout the halls had everything to do with reading and writing because it was familiar to me.

She offered to be his homework tutor. She would make sure his weekly homework folder was complete and watch and evaluate his progression one on one.

I happily agreed. I dreaded the "weekly homework folder," and I was relieved she offered to help. Maybe she could give me some insight as she worked with him.

She became a team player with me and a teaching mentor, and together we ensured Douglas received an education that allowed him to shine on stage and in the classroom.

She immediately noticed homework was a problem because if my son wrote for too long, he would be physically sick. I knew that, and she validated the issue.

Working closely with his teacher, I could see she had the same experiences I had with Doug. We became very close friends, and I finally shared with her that I believed my son had the same problems as my husband: dyslexia and dysgraphia.

She had never heard of those conditions, and we both concluded it was time to have my son independently tested.

The results were baffling to both of us.

My son (and later my daughter) was deemed *twice-exceptional*: above average IQ (in the gifted range), but well below average when it came to writing and reading.

Nobody knew the best way for my son to learn reading and writing, so I studied everything I could on the subject. That's how I came to understand the concept of the four types of learners:

- Traditional learners
- Gifted learners
- Learners with invisible learning differences
- Twice-exceptional (2e) learners

Public schools are not designed to teach non-traditional learners. They provide a standardized approach that they expect all the children to follow. It's very rigid, and it's also difficult for teachers and administrators inside the system to modify or adapt the curriculum to meet each child's needs.

Each type of learner has their own strengths and challenges. For this reason, you can't use the same teaching methods with all learners and expect the same results.

Yet, that's how our school system is built. And even traditional learners suffer under these conditions.

Traditional Learners

The **traditional learners** are the kids who follow along and fit squarely in the school system. They are considered the "easy" kids and the ones that teachers want in their classes.

Traditional learners are the students most General Education teachers are teaching to. They are the students who learn by memorization and reciting techniques. They fit inside the standard educational box, but unfortunately, a lot of these students are also slipping through the cracks. They aren't receiving a full and rich education because of large class sizes and the mandatory "teach to the test" culture in American classrooms.

While they perform well on standardized tests, they benefit from enriching their critical thinking, problem-solving, and decision-making skills—skills at which homeschooling excels. The traditional learning students blossom and rapidly advance when they have individualized programs that allow them to progress at their own pace and explore their interests.

It allows the parent to act as a facilitator to their child's learning, and it permits the child to dig deep to find the knowledge themselves rather than simply being told the information from a book.

Gifted Kids

The **gifted kids** have high IQs. Intellectually, they are much more advanced than the other students. They need a specialized curriculum as well as a plan in place that focuses on social skills with peers their own age.

Unfortunately, in many public school classrooms, they tend to separate the gifted kids from the Gen Ed class to put them on an advanced academic track, but that removes the child from the opportunity to interact with their peers their own age. These kids have an advanced intellectual mind, but they are still chronologically their age and maturity level. They need situations to learn social cues and master life skills, which are extremely important, and homeschooling provides children many creative opportunities for gifted kids to foster peer relationships.

Learners with Invisible Learning Differences (ILDs)

When I started my career as a Montessori teacher for ages 6-9, I changed my use of learning disabilities to invisible learning differences.

I use "difference" because "disability" implies inherent inability. "Difference" puts the onus on the educators to adapt their teaching methods.

These are learning differences that aren't obvious, such as dyslexia, dysgraphia, dyspraxia, dyscalculia, or ADHD, etc. As a result, children with invisible learning differences may be labeled as lazy or not trying hard enough with their academics.

This creates low self-esteem with the child, and they may become disruptive during class time. The behavioral problems begin because nobody addresses the academic difficulties.

The **kids with invisible learning differences** start the school year prepared to be disappointed and may feel defeated. Before they come to class, they may already be labeled as a "disruptive kid" or "problem kid."

If school is creating daily stress, then the benefits of the school environment become non-existent and detrimental to the family unit, the child's self-esteem, and mental health. When parents call me about their child with invisible learning differences, they feel defeated because school affects family dynamics.

My biggest talent in the classroom was finding the child's unique talents, gifts, and learning styles. That's the expertise I bring to my Maverick Homeschool Method.

Showing parents how to create an independent plan that addresses their child's academic differences is essential to progress efficiently, and finding programs to highlight their abilities boosts their self-esteem and promotes a love of learning.

The 7 Main Types of Learning Disabilities as Classified by Learning Disabilities Association of America

Dyslexia – A language processing disorder that impacts writing, reading, and reading comprehension.

Dysgraphia – A learning disability characterized by difficulties with writing and other fine motor skills. Handwriting and spelling are often affected.

Dyscalculia – A learning disability that causes trouble with math at many levels. For example, those with dyscalculia may struggle with understanding key concepts like greater than versus less than.

Auditory processing disorder – A learning disability that causes difficulty with processing sounds. The brain misinterprets the information received by the ears.

Language processing disorder (LPD) – A subset of auditory processing disorder. Individuals with LPD have specific challenges with processing spoken language and is defined by the Learning Disabilities Association of America as "difficulty attaching meaning to sound groups that form words, sentences, and stories."

Nonverbal learning disabilities (NVLD) – The name may indicate the inability to speak, but it refers to difficulties in understanding nonverbal behaviors and social cues from others such as body language, facial expression, tone, etc.

Visual perceptual/visual motor deficit – This learning disorder often manifests as poor hand-eye coordination, difficulty handling small instruments like pencils and scissors, losing one's place when reading, trouble navigating surroundings, and unusual eye activity when trying to follow words or motions.

Source: PlaygroundEquipment.com

Twice-exceptional (2e) Kids

The **twice-exceptional (2e) kids** have the intellectual abilities of gifted kids, but they have deficiencies in other areas, often around reading and writing. For example, my son Doug is twice-exceptional. He could hold an intellectual conversation about politics when he was three years old, but at the age of seven, he had trouble reading the word "cat."

Twice-exceptional kids are a mix of gifted kids and kids with invisible learning differences. These children are the most challenging for traditional schools and get tremendous benefits from home-schooling.

There is nothing in the school system that is designed to help them learn. Twice-exceptional kids are a rare phenomenon, and many schools have never seen children like them. So, they are unprepared to deal with them.

The biggest challenge with twice-exceptional kids is for teachers to understand that they are off the scale intellectually but are way below average in other areas. That makes twice-exceptional kids an anomaly for the traditional schooling system. The danger for these kids is for the school to say, "He/she is a brilliant kid. They'll figure it out on their own."

No, they won't.

Because twice-exceptional kids often have serious learning differences in reading and writing, schools want to put them in Special Ed. But since they are intellectually gifted, Special Ed teachers say they don't belong there. That becomes a conundrum for the school, and many of these children can fall through the cracks.

When I work with twice-exceptional kids, I identify where they are gifted and where they need more help. I tailor-build a student education plan (SEP) that leverages their specific gifts while supporting them where they face more challenges.

Famous 2e Personalities

Tom Cruise
Henry Winkler
Jay Leno
Whoopi Goldberg
Robin Williams
Stephen Hawking
Leonardo da Vinci
Albert Einstein
Pablo Picasso
Thomas Edison

More Challenges with My Daughter

My daughter Alexis, who is two years younger than Doug, didn't have dysgraphia, but her dyslexia appeared to be worse than her brother's, and she was also deemed 2e.

She is artistically gifted with above average intelligence but would write mirror-backward and had a severe lateral lisp. The lisp was so bad I sometimes had to be her interpreter for her teachers at school when she couldn't be understood. Eventually, it was corrected with speech therapy.

These learning differences were a struggle.

I decided to have my kids tested through the public school district. Their local district produced an Individual Education Plan to be implemented inside the classroom for both of my children.

We decided to give public school a chance. Unfortunately, for our family, the experience was a complete disaster.

I had to advocate for my kids with each teacher, and I had to make sure that the teachers were putting in place the accommodations and modifications outlined in the IEP.

The public school did not honor the IEPs and let my kids slip through the cracks.

IEP: Individual Education Plan: Lays out all the special education support that a child requires to succeed in the public school system. It contains the child's current strengths and needs, measurable goals to reach within a year, and the services to help the child meet those goals.

SEP: Student Education Plan: Homeschool version of an IEP/ISP

IDEA: Individuals with Disabilities Education Act: In 1990, a law passed that guaranteed children with special needs would receive a free and appropriate education with the accommodations and modifications tailored to their individual needs.

Section 504 of The Rehabilitation Act: Prohibits discrimination against children and ADULTS with disabilities in both public schools and other settings. The Rehabilitation Act

Why Choose Homeschooling?

If you look at the official statistics, the main drivers for adopting homeschooling are:

- The desire to provide religious instruction that isn't provided in government-sponsored schools.
- Concerns about the learning environment of district schools. This could run the gamut from intimidation and bullying to racism and physical violence.
- General dissatisfaction with academic teaching at other schools, including the curriculum offered, the breadth of activities provided, and the general teaching approach (sitting still for hours on end, for example).
- COVID has exposed many of these flaws in the public school system. Parents have seen first-hand how their kids live through their schooling, day in and day out. And many don't like it.
- It's part of the reason so many parents have turned to ***private*** homeschooling after the pandemic hit.

The Many Reasons to Homeschool Your Kids

While the reasons above cover a large portion of the population, here are many other reasons why you may want to homeschool your kids:

- You don't like what the public school system has to offer, but you can't afford a private school.
- Schools focus on meeting certain goals from which they can't deviate. It's a rigid system focused on testing and grading. With homeschooling, you have more flexibility, and you can focus on the love of learning instead of learning to pass a test.
- You can customize or individualize the curriculum and learning environment for each child in your house. What worked for one child may not be suitable for the next one.
- To protect your minority children from racism in public schools or lower expectations of children of color (e.g., Black) (e.g., Fields-Smith, 2020; Mazama & Lundy, 2012).[3]
- Your child no longer has to live with a "label" such as, "Special Ed kid," "ADHD kid," or "problem kid." He or she is just a child.
- You never have to deal with homework. You can do everything during the day.
- You get to spend more time with your child, which creates stronger and longer-lasting bonds.
- If you have more than one child in your home, homeschooling them all builds stronger relationships between siblings.
- Your house becomes a learning environment where all the tools you need are present (books, educational material, etc.). If you need or want specific material, you can get it yourself instead of waiting for the school to decide whether their budget allows it.
- You learn along with your child.
- There is less exposure to illnesses.
- You can adapt schooling to your work schedule instead of the other way around.

---

[3] www.nheri.org/research-facts-on-homeschooling/

- Your child can learn one-on-one instead of being forced to follow a group that may be moving along too quickly or too slowly.
- If your child has a silent learning disability, you can help them in ways that the traditional school system can't.
- You have a gifted kid who is bored at school or is neglected by the system.
- You want your child to think "outside of the box…" without being punished for it.
- You can meet and mingle with many other parents who share the same values as you.
- If your child has been bullied or otherwise belittled in school, their self-esteem and confidence may be shattered. You can rebuild that confidence with homeschooling.
- Your child learns life skills that are no longer taught in school. These are skills that they will use daily throughout their lives (cooking, maintaining a household, creating, and keeping a budget, etc.). Imagine, your child learns from doing their chores!
- You always know what your child is learning. If they have difficulties in their learning, you know about it first-hand, instead of hearing about it weeks or months later from the school.
- Learning is no longer something you only do outside your home. Instead, it becomes a way of life.
- Homeschooled kids do better in national tests and get better SAT and ACT scores than kids educated in the public or private school systems.
- From an academic point of view, you can do more than traditional schools.

- You can use as many teaching methods as you want. You aren't bound to a specific method or approach like most teachers in the school system.
- If another catastrophe like COVID-19 ever occurs, your child's schooling doesn't stop. You have an alternative at your disposal.

Yes, there are a lot of very good reasons why you would choose to homeschool your child. You probably have other reasons that I haven't listed. I'd love to hear about them!

What about academic performance?

If you have spoken to the people around you about homeschooling your kids, you may not have received an enthusiastic reception.

In fact, some people may have tried to dissuade you from homeschooling your kids, saying that they would not get as good an education as they would in the traditional school system.

Rest assured: They are wrong. You are making the right decision by deciding to homeschool your kids.

Here are some facts about homeschooled kids that most people don't know, courtesy of the National Home Education Research Institute:

- The home-educated typically score 15 to 30 percentile points above public-school students on standardized academic achievement tests. (The public-school average is the 50th percentile; scores range from 1 to 99.) A 2015 study found

Black homeschool students to be scoring 23 to 42 percentile points above Black public-school students (Ray, 2015).[4]

- The level of formal education of homeschooling parents or the family household income doesn't matter. Homeschooled students score higher on achievement tests than their public-school counterparts.
- Homeschooling parents don't need to be certified teachers for their kids to succeed academically.
- The government doesn't need to regulate homeschooling because it doesn't affect academic results.
- Colleges are increasingly actively recruiting children who come from a homeschooling background.

By now, you should be convinced that homeschooling is the best solution to create a great future for your child.

At this point, you should have your "why"—THE reason for you to implement homeschooling in your family.

With that, it's time to look at how you can do it in an effective and enjoyable way.

---

[4] www.nheri.org/research-facts-on-homeschooling/

SECTION 2

Specific Solutions

The Maverick Method of Homeschooling

My experience as a teacher and as the parent of children with invisible learning differences allowed me to develop what I call The Maverick Method of Homeschooling™.

It's based on all the happy—and not so happy—experiences I had while teaching children with invisible learning differences and homeschooling my children.

It's based on five principles.

Principle 1: You're never alone

When my children had difficulties in the traditional school system, I often felt like the district or the teachers abandoned me.

One example is when a teacher said that they didn't have to do anything for my son because he was brilliant enough to find a solution on his own.

In my head, I was thinking, "Not only is that *illegal*, but it's also *shameful*. The system is lazy." But I also understood their position.

It wasn't always their fault—they just were not equipped to deal with children who have invisible learning differences, are gifted, or are twice exceptional since the school system is made for traditional learners.

If your children don't fit the traditional learner mold, you may feel as if you have no support.

With The Maverick Method of Homeschooling, you are never alone.

You're not stuck teaching at the board all day like you see teachers in the traditional school system.

It's also not the COVID style of homeschooling, which is crisis homeschooling rather than real homeschooling.

Instead, my method leverages resources that give you the best experience possible.

Teaching is interactive, and children don't have to sit on a chair at a table without moving for seven hours a day.

The Maverick Method of Homeschooling takes the best of both worlds. It takes the best aspects of the school system and adds them to your homeschooling approach.

This allows you to integrate sports for the children who are athletic and performing arts for the children with artistic talent without needing to become an expert at either.

With so many families choosing to homeschool their kids, there is a community of homeschooling parents near you. These are people that have the same goals and ideals as you, and you can join them to get support.

Remember, I can guide you to find the support you seek.

Principle 2: Stress-free and fun

Learning doesn't need to be rigid to be academic. It can be free.

Rigidity causes stress, both in school and in life.

Traditional schooling within a district is very rigid. Teachers have specific rules to follow, and if they try to do anything out of the ordinary to help a child, they may get reprimanded.

With The Maverick Method of Homeschooling, you'll see how schooling can be freeing and flexible.

Teaching adapts to the style of the child, and you have the power to find the best method suited to your child. It's not a race, and kids are allowed to learn at their own pace. It doesn't matter if they take a few more months or even a few more years to learn what traditional learners do.

The goal is for them to learn and to love learning.

Principle 3: Freedom and flexibility

Homeschooling provides the best of both worlds.

As a parent, you take control of your child's education. You get to make sure that it's well-rounded and you focus on the whole child.

By having control of your child's education, you do what's best for them.

If your child is tired, you can stop teaching without being second-guessed. You can resume that lesson some other time. You won't be reprimanded because of that.

You don't have to follow the seven-hour sitting down approach that you learned in school or that teachers still use today.

You can decide to use a whole week to educate on a single topic. For example, let's say you decide to teach in a museum environment, so your child can see and feel what they are learning. Instead of doing a single half-day outing, you can go to the museum every day of the week.

It doesn't have to simply be a day trip. Each visit can focus on a different part of the museum.

It's also easier to adapt to real-life situations. Let me give you an example.

Let's imagine that you live in a region with no bus service, and you need to drive your child to school every day. One day the car breaks down. What happens?

You're not able to bring the kids to school, and nobody else can get them. Then, your child receives an unexcused absence, and the school piles up the work missed during the day, leaving the child with a day of learning lost, and overloaded the next with no real, meaningful learning happening.

With homeschooling, instead of having lost a day of learning and experience, you can use it as an opportunity to teach a life skill: mechanics.

Many schools don't teach these life skills anymore. You get to do that when you're homeschooling, and it makes your child better prepared to face real life.

By integrating your child's schooling with everyday activities, education becomes a family affair. Chores become learning experiences, skills that they will use and cherish for the rest of their lives.

You can't get that type of freedom and flexibility from traditional schooling.

Principle 4: Whole child focus

Homeschooling doesn't focus on labels. All labels are removed because you're just dealing with a child.

In traditional schooling, you have children with dyslexia, special needs kids, gifted kids, and so on.

With homeschooling, those labels are irrelevant. The child is unique, and the teaching approach is unique to that kid.

This allows you to integrate all types of learners and all types of learning approaches.

You can also incorporate extracurricular classes—sometimes even from your neighborhood school—like sports, art, or theater, etc.

It allows you to create a stress-free learning environment that both you, your child, and the entire family enjoy.

Principle 5: Family centered

With homeschooling, you have access to many different types of curricula that focus on the whole child, making it family-inclusive. This allows you to integrate life skills with learning.

You can do this creatively with everyday tasks. For example, children can learn about fractions while baking a cake with you. They can improve their math skills while learning to balance a checkbook or doing a household budget.

When they do these activities, they are contributing to the welfare of the family and that provides a great self-esteem boost.

When it comes to homeschooling, you have a wealth of methods to choose from.

You can pick the ones that work best for your family while taking into consideration your child's preferred learning methods, your responsibilities at home and at work, your location, whether you want to travel or stay in one place, and so on.

This removes schooling stress because learning is no longer a chore. It's a joy.

Academic Theater: Using the Arts to Remember

Throughout my teaching career, I realized the best way to have children memorize important academic information is through the arts.

Art is an all-on experience that engages the mind, the body, and the soul. It is essential to capture the imagination of children, and the arts is a way to reach all ranges of learners.

My hero is Ron Clark. He is an educator who started a non-profit school based in southeast Atlanta, Georgia for kids grades 4th-8th. Ron Clark's philosophy for learning is having core subjects infused with music and the performing arts. The students are encouraged to get on their chairs and desks to sing and express the information they learn through the joy of music and movement.

I admired Ron Clark's philosophy so much I implemented the same methods inside my classroom, academic enrichment programs, and now my homeschool methods. If you can get the kids moving, happy about what they're doing, and excited about their academic lessons, then learning even the most challenging subjects is no longer painful. It's no longer a pain for anyone—not the kid, educator, or parents.

I realize from my classroom experience that music, movement, learning lines, poems, songs, and utilizing fine art to retain facts and information are the best way to do well in the academic arena. This is especially true for kids with an invisible learning disability, but it translates to everybody. So, when parents investigate a more personalized education approach, I recommend parents focus on programs in their neighborhood homeschool community with academic-based enrichment lessons focusing on the arts.

Getting kids on the "same sheet of music"

Let's take singing, for example. It's a tool I often used to help kids learn and retain information.

I remember when my students would take my exams, I would often hear them humming and tapping their feet because that's how they recalled the information.

I believe it all starts with a child's learning environment. A personalized homeschool academic enrichment program with virtual classes, co-ops, and homeschool umbrella programs utilizes a creative and artistic approach for every child and every learning style.

Knowing the correct programs to use for an individualized homeschool plan infusing the performing arts inside every subject (science, history, math, or language arts) is easy to create, and remember, there are professionals available to guide you through the process.

Teaching topics through the arts is always beneficial. The kids enjoy it so much, and you will catch them singing the songs, and parents, you'll get into it, too! Once again, it builds on the home base classroom family structure. The best part is that the kids remember the information. It's all about grabbing and keeping their attention.

Using songs to learn and recall is not new. I remember learning reading and math skills in the 70s and 80s with educational programming on TV.

Think of "Schoolhouse Rock." They have songs about legislation (*I'm Just a Bill*), grammar (*Conjunction Junction*), science (*Electricity, Electricity*), finance (*Dollars and Sense*), and more.

Today, years later, I still remember all those songs. You probably remember a few, too!

And this was on TV! Imagine bringing that same philosophy to your child's learning every day. How much of an impact can it have? It can be life changing.

Creating an independent homeschooling program using enrichment services and extracurricular activities allows children to experience being a part of a more extensive community. Kids become proficient in musical instruments, become part of a band, and learn fine arts. They participate in full theater shows and choir performances. Families take field trips to local museums and historical sites with their local homeschooling community.

Many enrichment centers have creative academic classroom methods and incorporate project and hands-on learning opportunities for all the subjects. There are garden classes, cooking classes, experiment-based science classes, musical history classes, etc. Everything is done throughout the day and continues to flow into the next day. Parents get to decide the level of homework to give their child. Some parents want extra work after school hours; others don't. The beauty of taking charge of your child's education is that you, the parent, make that decision.

Academic Theater and Sports to Expand the Impact of Every Child's Learning

Academic theater and sports help on the social level as well as the academic level.

That enthusiasm from a play performance or a soccer game transfers from the activity to their playdates and interacting with peers positively.

A plan that develops lasting friendships that evolve through enrichment programs and co-op classes are essential for reinforcing children's learning. The kids can practice their skills together, bring families together, and solidify the home-based philosophy.

Academic enrichment theater integrates the four levels of learners in the classroom because they're all engaged on a common goal. There isn't a competition to get the highest grade, finish first, or anything like that.

The kids help each other along the way.

Using Art to Engage Every Kid at Their Ability

The Montessori philosophy says that kids *experience* learning as much as they learn from a book or from somebody teaching them.

In the previous chapter, I explained how Academic Theater helps kids remember information and sparks creative learning.

That's based on the experiential learning philosophy of the Montessori approach.

I love creating musicals and plays, and I incorporate them for every aspect of learning for every subject. When I am unable to write my own plays, I rely on a company called Bad Wolf Press.[5]

Bad Wolf Press has many wonderful academic-based musicals, which complement any homeschool academic enrichment program or co-op group.

Theater isn't the only way. Infusing all types of arts into your individual academic homeschooling plan gives kids as many avenues as possible to show what they can do, and they shine in the process.

---

[5] https://www.badwolfpress.com/

Alternative Approaches - Private School Options

Are you looking for something outside the box but not necessarily wanting to jump into homeschooling? Looking for a private school with an unconventional and alternative approach to education?

You can find many existing approaches, and each has their strengths and weaknesses. Some examples of alternative education approaches are:

- **Amara Berri:** This system employs methods, including games, to help students learn. The goal is for them to develop competencies in a more exploratory way. Teachers act as guides alongside their students, respecting each student's own individual learning pace and potential.

- **Doman**: Doman is a learning ecosystem with a focus on students' individuality and development. They strive to challenge them and encourage them to grow. They use natural, spontaneous learning methods that target the physical, intellectual, emotional, and social aspects of human development.

- **Harkness:** In Harkness classrooms, students sit with their classmates and teachers at a Harkness table to discuss a diverse range of topics. The discussions are often deep and wide-ranging, touching on subjects such as calculus to history. The Harkness method is a far cry from the traditional classroom setup of a teacher standing in front of rows of desks lecturing to passive students. At the Harkness table, individuals have time to develop their opinions and share them with the rest of the class. The teacher's main responsibility is to make sure no one dominates and that everyone stays on topic.

- **Montessori**: Montessori education is a way of teaching children how to learn. It emphasizes freedom, independence, and creativity in a nurturing environment.

- **Reggio Emilia**: This methodology says that children learn by being the protagonist in their own learning. This is best done with their teachers as guides who help to enhance their curiosity. Classrooms are designed to promote diverse practices that allow students to enjoy their identity and purpose. Parents play a vital role in shaping these experiences.

- **Sudbury**: In Sudbury schools, students are given complete autonomy when it comes to determining what to learn and how they'll do it. The Sudbury philosophy says that students should be able to make their own decisions and choose a certain level of responsibility for themselves. If they make bad decisions, they learn by dealing with the consequences.

- **Waldorf**: Waldorf education is a humanistic approach to curriculum and instruction, emphasizing creativity, imagination, artistic beauty, and practical life skills.

While I only mention these methods, there are many more that I don't have the space to cover in this book. When consulting with parents, I look at all the options (public, private, and homeschool). I match the educational methods best suited to their children. Importantly, it is the power to choose what is best for your child and having the freedom to create the most productive educational path for your child and family.

The great thing is that these alternative approaches used in private schools can easily be implemented in a homeschool plan. The choice is yours to make!

Famous Successful People Who Were Homeschooled

- Serena and Venus Williams
- Albert Einstein
- Taylor Swift
- Emma Watson
- The Jonas Brothers
- Simone Biles
- Tim Tebow
- Ryan Gosling
- Justin Timberlake

Hiring an educational consultant to find your child the ideal learning environment is a great time saver. The research of an educational consultant provides families information and connects them with programs that fit the specific needs of their children.

The Montessori Method

I taught in a Montessori classroom for over a decade, and the reward from the experiential, hands-on learning was magical for all my students.

To give you a sense of how these specialized teaching methods can be incorporated into your homeschooling program, here are a few examples.

Montessori Lesson Example: Botany

The Montessori method develops children's emotions about the universe and mother nature, and teaching botany introduces the environment to the children. I always loved teaching botany in my Montessori classroom, which crosses over to my homeschooling methods. The botany lesson teaches children the system of scientific classification with materials called the Five Kingdom Chart and the Plant Classification Chart. The class begins with life cycles and emphasizes the importance of plants for humans and animal life. The lessons magnify the importance of sustainability and educate children to protect the earth and fragile ecosystems. My classes always begin in the garden; growing your food can happen in any space and is essential for the Montessori philosophy.

We begin our outdoor lessons and walk the perimeter of the space, and instead of putting a picture up and stating, "It's a tree," the Montessori approach focuses on an experiential approach.

The children find real trees, feel the bark, and trace it on the paper. They identify the trees by looking at the roots and the leaves. But it doesn't stop there: They also explain their observations.

For kids who have trouble spelling, this approach is excellent because it allows them to show what they know without being stopped by the writing barrier.

Montessori lessons transition nicely in a homeschool setting. You use one activity to allow each child to work to the level of their current ability. The more advanced kids can choose to write a creative story about the tree or write a report about the scientific parts of the tree, and other children can decide to paint a picture of the tree. The creativity and critical thinking are endless. Maria Montessori's methods are for both parent and child to progress academically with natural exploration and investigative skill.

Montessori Lesson Example: Creative Writing

Even though some of my students had writing difficulties, I still used creative writing as a learning tool. Maria Montessori encouraged children to tell oral stories as part of the creative writing activity. There are opportunities through learning other subjects for an extension of the creative writing lesson. An example is with my daughter. She was using the sandpaper letters and tracing the letter P, and she began to talk about her stuffed rabbit in her room named Peter. Then she drew a picture of the story to show me the action. She was pre-reading, so she told me her story, and I scribed her words. She then copied her own story underneath the drawing that began her idea, which is a big part of the Montessori method regarding creative writing.

So, every day I presented a picture to the kids and asked them to write about it. Some kids started with writing, but others began with drawing. I never squashed their creativity on how to deliver their creative writing story. The Montessori methodology allows the kids the freedom to imagine allowing impromptu stories to happen without rigid writing rules getting in their way. It is a wonderful homeschooling approach to writing.

Montessori Reading Method: Great for Homeschooling

Reading happens organically with the Montessori pedagogy. For children with reading issues, the Montessori method allows the child to learn at their own pace. Interestingly enough, reading begins with writing with Montessori; children explore the Montessori letter manipulatives and put them together to see how the letters and sounds, when strung together, create words. When children write phonetically, they begin to recognize phonetic sounds to specific letters then words.

The Montessori method is a great homeschool tool for struggling readers because it follows their skill, ability, and individual pace. The Montessori technique combined with the Orton Gillingham method helped ease my kids' reading difficulty due to their dyslexia and dysgraphia. Although reading flow didn't begin for them until much later than their peers, these two philosophies and practices gave them the foundation to tackle reading independently eventually.

The Montessori method provides these types of creative approaches to learning—and more as we'll see in the next chapter.

Some Alternative Education Statistics

- There were an estimated 5 million homeschooling families in the United States during March of 2021, which represent about 8 million students.
- Homeschooling saves about $68 billion for taxpayers.
- In 2016, 80% of households who chose to homeschool did it because of concerns over the learning environment of traditional education institutions.
- There are 20,000 Montessori schools worldwide, 3,000 are AMI accredited in the USA, and there are many more private schools and homeschools that use the philosophy inside the

classroom without being AMI accredited. There are 560 Montessori public schools—district, magnet, and charters.

- A study at the University of Virginia shows that Montessori learning reduces the learning gap between underperforming low-income students and those from higher-income families.

- Children who graduate from Montessori programs outperform children from traditional schools in many abilities.

- There are about 130 Waldorf schools in the United States.

- A study of Waldorf education showed that Waldorf schools underperformed district schools in lower grades K–3 for reading and math. This is because they do not have children begin the reading process until second or third grade. However, by seventh and eighth grades, those same schools outperformed district schools in those same areas.

- A study of Waldorf schools in Germany showed that Waldorf students were more enthusiastic about learning and less bored in school.

- 83% of unschooling students pursue some form of higher education.

- Studies show unschooled learners enter careers in STEM, the arts, and pursue entrepreneurship as adults.

- According to the U.S. Department of Education, one study shows that 41% of homeschool students are Black, Asian, Hispanic, and non-White/non-Hispanic. This highlights a fast-growing popularity among minorities.

- Private Homeschooling families do not depend on public, tax-funded resources to educate their children.

Sources: Health Research Funding, Montessori-Science.org, The Research Institute for Waldorf Education, University of Virginia, Resilient Educator, National Home Education Research Institute.

Activity-Based Learning/ Teaching

Let's talk a bit about math.

We've seen how performing arts allow the kids to learn about history and science. We can also teach grammar using the same approach. These subjects work well because the information is memory-based.

But math is a bit different. While there is some memory-based information in math, a lot of it requires understanding.

That's where the Montessori method really shines for a home-school setting.

Montessori Example: Teaching Math

The Montessori homeschool math curriculum provides children with incremental opportunities to explore mathematical solutions by assuring exposure to concrete manipulatives. When a child can touch and hold the materials representative of a numerical problem presented to them, it allows them to work on more abstract concepts later as they progress forward. Each concrete manipulative used in a Montessori learning environment evolves as time moves forward. They master each concept until they no longer rely on it, moving on to finding solutions on paper or in their head.

Montessori Math Materials for Hands-on Activities

Montessori manipulatives allow the kids to visually learn concrete mathematical operations. One example is placement value: Manipulatives (educational tools that children can literally "manipulate" with their hands) help them understand the difference between hundreds, tens, and single-digit units.

This is beneficial for the kids that suffer from dyscalculia. Children that have dyscalculia may exhibit other challenges:

- They have trouble with verbal directions, reading maps.
- They have difficulty understanding the concept of time.
- They have trouble understanding the difference between right and left.
- While it can be a dyslexic problem, tying their shoes is also a problem for kids with dyscalculia.

Parents need to be aware of these difficulties. Knowing the signs of a math learning disability early on allows parents to research and pick the appropriate curriculum to create a supportive math learning environment for the child, with different ways to successfully absorb the essential information to progress at their own pace.

Montessori homeschool math has children create board games using geometrical shapes, bead bars, and playdough. Montessori Counting games for young children are hands-on; the children work with a number board, arithmetic board, and numeral decomposition board.

The Montessori philosophy works so well with homeschooling children at all levels of learning, not just children with invisible learning differences. A favorite Montessori math activity is the stamp game. It is a box with sections and small colored tiles. They are different colors; the green tiles represent ones, the blue tiles describe tens, the red tiles represent hundreds, and then thousands are represented by darker green tiles. The stamp game material teaches addition, subtraction, multiplication, and even division into the thousands. The more advanced kids will begin multiplication and division games. They keep moving forward, eventually learning algebraic concepts at a young age.

For additional creative math-building activities, children can make a 3D math game using dominos. Children can make math games with dice and number stamps.

The wonderful hands-on activities are limitless when creating homeschool math learning.

The Importance of Having Fun While Learning

Learning should be fun; it shouldn't be a struggle. Even those who struggle to understand should have fun learning. If you don't enjoy learning, you will try to avoid learning altogether. And if you don't keep learning until the day you die, that's a wasted life.

If you make learning enjoyable, the kids can't wait to learn, even if they have an invisible learning difference.

I make sure that the kids I work with are always at a level where they can learn. It's never entirely out of their grasp.

The information sticks using these methods.

That's the point of my maverick teaching approach.

Peer-to-Peer Teaching in Your Homeschool

Peer-to-peer teaching is a critical approach with all kids but especially with children with invisible learning differences. I've used peer-to-peer teaching in my mixed-aged classrooms and have had tremendous success. In your homeschool, this translates to older siblings teaching younger siblings.

It takes a bit of time to get the process going because children aren't used to being in the driver's seat and leading a learning session with a sibling/peer. This technique is something to be practiced and guided by the facilitator, whether that is a parent, tutor, or enrichment educator.

The goal is not to offload the teaching responsibilities to the students. Instead, it's to let students use their gifts to the fullest and share that gift with other children with more difficulties in that area.

With peer-to-peer learning, we are also satisfying a child's desire to be helpful toward others. When given the chance, children can be very generous, and they feel good about sharing. As parents and educators, we want to build on that innate desire.

Once the children are used to working together, the learning groove begins, and the magic happens.

Modeling the Facilitator

Some children often finish an academic task before their siblings.

Instead of piling more busywork on them (like giving them more worksheets), I will recommend that parents have their older children assist their younger siblings during work time. Locating or creating a homeschooling group is helpful, so their children can help other students during a working session/block.

When a child helps another child with their schoolwork and learns how to direct the student to the information to research the answers themselves, it also helps the older students' critical thinking and processing skills. Now, they start to understand the process of teaching vs. giving out the answers.

Kids should pretend to be the teacher when assisting a sibling or other children with academic activities. More specifically, they should pretend to be the parent/tutor/private teacher/enrichment educator. Observe how they guide learning. Do they teach by asking questions? They discover asking questions is the best way to learn.

The Flow Between Gifted Children and Peers

I've talked mostly about children with invisible learning differences, 2e (twice exceptional), and traditional learners, but gifted kids have their own set of challenges.

Many gifted kids spend a lot of time with children several years older although that has its benefits—the chronological age of a gifted child may be seven years old but has an intellectual mind of a twelve-year-old. However, emotionally and socially, they are still seven and need interaction from peers their age, but that can be hard when they don't do many things together. Still, a twelve-year-old's academic mind makes it easier to talk with older kids, so becoming a facilitator of learning for their peers brings opportunities for connection and friendships and even deepens the relationship with their siblings. The kids start to enjoy each other's company in an academic homeschool setting.

An enrichment class, or co-op program, gives kids at all levels an opportunity to teach each other. They can help by scribing for younger children, helping them look things up in a book, read to them, and so on.

I encourage parents to talk about differences in learning early on during the educational process with your child. Children need to know everyone has special gifts and are just as intelligent as the other kids no matter their learning style.

Strengthening Bonds

Over the school year, siblings will have been helping each other academically. The neighborhood homeschooling children help one another during your child's academic enrichment classes, so this learning philosophy becomes a natural part of the classroom/ homeschool family.

Having the kids teach each other creates friendships that, otherwise, wouldn't have been possible. It positively influences the kids, allowing them to give each child additional information in different ways, and homeschooling provides many opportunities to create that style of peer-to-peer teaching.

There is no longer a feeling of superiority with the levels of learning because some kids don't learn the same way others do. In a traditional school, teachers tend to single out kids with learning differences; that spills over onto the playground with peers bullying them about their academic difficulties in the classroom. It doesn't happen in the homeschooling community because families facilitate the learning, create the classroom environment, and direct peer-to-peer learning methods without time restrictions.

In environments where the kids with invisible learning differences are singled out, it makes them angry and humiliated. When you belittle them, it doesn't encourage learning—they don't get that "I can't wait to do this again" feeling.

Everyone has something unique to offer that everyone can learn from. It's just a different style of learning. One group will have something to offer that the other group doesn't and vice versa.

The kids can really experience and learn from each other which leads to stronger relationships.

With the student interaction, all four groups of learners end up helping each other in different ways.

Nobody is left out of the learning process.

Homeschooling Multiple Ages and Learning Differences

In a homeschooling environment, you are often dealing with children of multiple ages and learning differences. It requires patience and dedication and sometimes learning to deal with situations that don't appear in a regular classroom (like sibling rivalry).

A Maverick Approach for Kids with Invisible Learning Differences

Traditional learning and curriculum focus on things I don't. For example, I'm not a big testing proponent. Test scores have taken over and now rule classrooms across America. I get phone calls from parents with children who have ILDs wanting an educational consultation to guide a test-free or limited testing academic program that focuses on the whole child learning model instead of teaching to the test. Testing culture is not useful for any kid navigating the learning experience, but it especially hurts the learning progression for kids with invisible learning differences. Creating the perfect individualized programs tailored to their child's interests, learning style, gifts, talents, and passions, NOT TESTS, can be accomplished with the help of an educational manager.

Create Momentum with Small Wins

I always recommend for parents to focus on highlighting the small wins for each mastery and celebrate each academic victory and build up momentum, so they have the confidence to conquer fears, insecurities and have the self-esteem to climb the mountain of success.

That's where the performing arts, other forms of talent, and creation come into play. The arts are not the only way to reach a child. Sports and volunteering in the community have a huge impact and focus on education for the whole child and deepen the home-based classroom family.

Engaging Kids with Invisible Learning Differences Using the Arts and Sports

One of the challenges with all kids, but especially children with invisible learning differences, is bringing them out of their shells, but it's not just them. Some kids are timid naturally. In both cases, the challenge is to make them overcome their fears when it comes to something new that they've never tried before. The performing arts is a great way to do that, and I help families facilitate those experiences in various ways to engage.

For example, I had one child while I was teaching an academic homeschool enrichment program, David, who would hide under a table and cover his ears with his hands when we began the musical aspect of the theater production. I believe he had sensory issues, and I turned down the music and let him be, but over time, he gradually took his hands off his ears and paid closer attention to what was going on with the rest of the children.

I offered him the stage manager role, where he could oversee what was happening. I told him that he could offer critiques and suggestions to make the academic play better.

At first, he would tell me—as an aside—what he thought the kids should do. Then, as time went by, he became more assertive with his suggestions until he eventually asked to participate in the play.

So, by putting no pressure on David, these little wins gave him more confidence and eventually allowed him to join the rest of the group. It is another example of how a homeschool enrichment program once or twice a week can make a world of difference with self-esteem and positive peer interaction.

What about IEPs? (Individual Education Plan)

I am an IEP parent coach and advocate for parents and their children. An IEP can be complex and scary for families to navigate, and I help guide parents through the IEP process.

The public-school teachers often don't have the training to properly teach children with IEPs, so they often aren't implemented correctly. It makes the parents mad and frustrates the teachers.

Many teacher-education programs offer just one class about students with disabilities to their general-education teachers, "Special Ed 101," as it's called at one New Jersey college. It's not enough to equip teachers for a roomful of children who can range from the gifted to students who read far below grade level due to a learning disability. A study in 2007 found that General Education teachers in a teacher-preparation program reported taking an average of <u>1.5 courses</u> focusing on inclusion or special education, compared to about 11 courses for special-education teachers. Educators say little has changed since then.[6]

---

[6] Source: Jackie Mader writes for The Hechinger Report,
www.theatlantic.com/education/archive/2017/03/
how-teacher-training-hinders-special-needs-students/518286/

This makes teaching children with invisible learning differences difficult if not impossible for mainstream teachers working in a traditional classroom.

Although changes in teacher training for special education children in the general education classroom are improving in some parts of the country, it is still minimal for most current public-school teachers. Children with invisible learning differences, otherwise known as SLD (specific learning disabilities), continue to fall through the cracks daily, affecting their overall future. The training for general education teachers for an inclusive classroom for kids with learning disabilities has a long way to go before the gap in classroom learning is closed.

The system is complicated, and when a family has a child that has an IEP implementation meeting to address their child's academic progress and their difficulties, it can be scary for everyone involved. These meetings can get very contentious, and parents call me for a consultation to review their child's IEP or hire me to advocate for their child by writing the appropriate letters, or they may have me attend their child's IEP meeting. I believe in working together with teachers and administrators. It is always the last resort to get lawyers involved. Developing a positive relationship with the IEP team helps the child and the family.

It's a difficult situation for teachers when they have students with many different learning styles and students with different needs.

For example, twice-exceptional kids are thrown from Gifted classes to Special Ed then back to regular classes because they don't belong anywhere in the educational system.

That's what happened to my son.

Douglas tested gifted, so he went into a program called GATE: gifted and talented education.

When he started, he couldn't read and write, so they sent him to Special Ed.

In Special Ed, they said he was too advanced, so they didn't want him.

Kids like him with Invisible Learning Differences (ILD) get lost in a system not designed for them. IEP advocates can help parents navigate that situation. They are for families whose kids don't have a place in the school system.

I recommend when the district simply isn't helping the child academically, socially, or emotionally, to look at other options. It is possible to turn their IEP to an ISP (Individualized Service Plan) for transitioning to private schools or you can turn your child's IEP to a SEP (Student Education Plan) for privately homeschooling purposes. Customizing an individualized homeschool program conducive to learning, progress, and success makes academic progress efficient, stress-free, and successful for kids with invisible learning differences.

Your school district may have given your child an IEP, but it may not be working, which is what drives parents of kids with special needs to seek a better way through homeschooling. Advocates and parent IEP coaches help you navigate your child's IEP meetings and progress. They will help transition your child over to homeschooling successfully and seamlessly. After all, most of them have been in your shoes and know the drill.

Taking charge of your child's education allows you the freedom to select the best learning style and environment and prepare kids for an independent, victorious future. My two adult children are now thriving in their field of choice. All we parents want for our children is their happiness and for them to live independently as adults. I found our unique family way, and I encourage you to find someone to guide your family to find your unique educational path as well.

Homeschooling Success: A Case Study

If you want complete power to educate your kids, you need to take your power back. I can show you how to do that, and this is what it can look like.

When I took a wonderful, bright student named Alyssa under my wing for the second time in my career, she was starting ninth grade.

I was Alyssa's second-grade teacher and have known her family for almost two decades. I taught her older sister in theater years before Alyssa ended up in my second-grade class.

I identified learning differences right away and discussed them with her parents because identifying and acting on those early signs is crucial.

I got her tested through the district, and she qualified for an IEP, and the private school honored it, which worked well for her in elementary school. Then, I got pregnant and left the school she attended, and I decided to homeschool my older children, so I did not see her or her family again until 4 years later.

The family had left the private school, and Alyssa began attending their local public school. Eventually, they reached out to me after a horrendous and unproductive eighth-grade IEP meeting.

The IEP meeting at the end of the 8th grade was disastrous. The school claimed that she would not graduate and that they could do nothing more for her academically. Her mom called me in a panic, asking for my help.

I was horrified by their experience and wanted to take the district to court, but the family simply wanted solutions, and I was the educator they were seeking.

Her parents wanted to move forward for their daughter's happiness, health, and education.

Her family became my educational teammates. We created a learning environment with homeschooling that mirrored a classroom family and co-op programs focused on her talents, gifts, and strengths. They hired me as Alyssa's educational home-school manager.

As an educational homeschool manager, I crafted an individualized curriculum with specialized classes and lessons for Alyssa's yearly academic high school calendar, ensuring that it was well balanced.

With Alyssa, I began with compassion because I could see she was traumatized by the same system that was supposed to protect her. So, her parents and I focused on her self-esteem first and foremost.

Did Alyssa have a language processing learning difference that prevented her from obtaining information the same way as traditional learning students? Yes.

But does that mean she doesn't deserve the same rights to education as everyone else? Of course not! She deserves the same rights to an equal education as everyone else.

Federal laws like IDEA (Individuals with Disabilities Education Act) and FAPE (Free Appropriate Public Education) tend to agree with me. Still, her parents chose to move forward with my maverick homeschool teaching style that worked for my family and other students, and I happily agreed.

So, the wonderful yellow brick road of learning began. Alyssa immediately blossomed and began to flourish with the individualized program I developed.

The plan included a homeschool umbrella program, enrichment co-op programs, trips to museums, online self-paced assignments, and hands-on project-based learning.

When COVID-19 suddenly happened and the world stopped, my educational management skills allowed me to adapt immediately. I molded meaningful education to Alyssa's individualized learning during an uncertain time.

I am proud to say that Alyssa had one of the most fruitful learning years of her academic career. She thrived and succeeded while students around the world struggled.

Her family is very proud of her success, and Alyssa's sense of self and confidence soared. She graduates in June 2022 with her high school diploma and a Teacher's Assistant certificate.

She has a big, beautiful, successful future ahead of her.

IEP advocates and educational consultants, and managers are here to help families take charge of their child's education.

What about ceremonies and traditions? Graduation? Prom?

If you are homeschooling through your child's public charter school, the school will most likely provide the ceremonies expected with schools like proms and graduations. They host dances and graduation ceremonies for grades K, 6th, 8th, and high school.

Private homeschools (PSA) or (PSS) have begun hosting statewide high school proms; in 2004, California joined them. Now the state hosts a homeschool prom each year, like Florida, New Jersey, and Ohio. Those huge events have sparked smaller private Umbrella Schools to sponsor and host proms and other dances locally. Parent committees plan customized dinners, and neighborhood home-school co-ops add special group events to enhance the overall homeschooling experience for kids and a sense of community for parents.

Public school districts do not grant graduation ceremonial privi-leges or diplomas to private homeschoolers. Still, most Umbrella schools (PSS) host beautiful graduation ceremonies, parent-child banquets, grad night trips, and award ceremonies for their home-school families. They host overseas trips and award each student a school diploma at the end of kindergarten, 6th, 8th, and 12th grades. These can be large events, or co-op homeschooling (PSA) families can choose to have smaller, more intimate moving-on ceremonies. It depends on what you choose for your family and based on your child's needs.

Do Colleges Accept Homeschool Students?

Homeschoolers have steadily outperformed their public school peers when taking standardized tests, like the SAT or ACT. Home-schooled students score about 72 points higher than the National Scholastic Aptitude Test (SAT) average. The average American College Test (ACT) score is 21. The average score for homeschool-ers is 22.8 out of a possible 36 points. Homeschoolers are at the 77th percentile on the Iowa Test of Basic Skills.[7]

These findings have been shown in states throughout the US, leading colleges not to require accredited high school diplomas for admission into their institutions. Each university has different requirements, which allows the child to prepare and focus on what they need to apply for. Many seniors prepare a detailed academic portfolio and take the GED or the high school proficiency exam. Others prepare and study for the standardized tests (ACT or SAT, or both) for admissions to colleges. Many students focus on their writing skills to ace college admissions essays because they are essential for college applications.

Both my 2e children are gifted in the arts, and they decided to focus on the top-performing arts colleges and fine arts colleges in

---

[7] https://wehavekids.com/education/
Do-Homeschoolers-Really-Do-Better-on-Tests

the country. These universities do not rely on standardized testing for admissions, but they focus on auditions and art portfolio submissions to make their final acceptance decision. I recommend parents look at the application requirements of the colleges their children are interested in applying to years in advance to prepare their child's direction after high school. No matter what college your child decides to apply to, they will need a high school transcript to move forward with any college application. Be sure to look over the state requirements to help determine all the essential classes your child will need to complete to apply.

If you file as a PSA, parents can use many templates to create their child's transcripts and a high school diploma. A great resource is HSLDA; they help you on your journey when you need to create report cards and transcripts, and they have many other resources available to PSA families.[8]

If you file with a PSS or Umbrella homeschool, they create the report cards and transcripts for you, and colleges or other schools can request your child's school records through them.

An educational consultant can help guide you with those educational choices.

Does my homeschooled child NEED to go to college to be a successful adult?

Parents ask me if their child must go to college to have a successful life? The easy answer is no. Many people have carved a very successful life without a college degree. We have all heard of Bill

---

[8] https://hslda.org/

Gates, Steve Jobs, Larry Ellison, etc., and they made it big without college degrees, but can everyone attain success? The answer is yes. In fact, with the internet and online learning at your fingertips, you can study your interests and become an expert without the burden of costly student loans. Many consulting jobs do not need a degree to begin in the chosen area of expertise, and entrepreneurship needs nothing but an idea, passion, and knowledge in your field to form a start-up. Often, young adults enter colleges not knowing what to focus on and shift from one academic major to another. With the rapid advancement of civilization, a 4-year degree can be obsolete by the time of graduation. Then, people find themselves unemployed and deep in debt.

A 4-year institution focuses on theoretical concepts, and students can't always apply the theories from lectures in the classroom in the real world. Vocational schools are an excellent option to choose other than a 4-year university. Young people can focus on relevant skills in half the time and have a higher chance of graduating. Trade schools have smaller class sizes, flexible schedules, and hands-on training. Most students from vocational schools transition directly to their career choice after graduation because their career services at these schools are excellent. Many students from trade school have a higher employment rate after graduation.

So, again, there are many different choices to choose from, and the great thing is you don't have to suffer or worry about what others think during the process because homeschooling focuses on what is best for the child. Freedom to educate independently is revolutionary! The choice is yours and your child's!

You are capable of homeschooling your child successfully!

Homeschooling my two eldest children and now my youngest makes me feel proud. I reject apprehension about homeschooling. Children have exceptional qualities. Kids have extraordinary talents that, when fostered, make children feel confident to share their unique gifts with the world. A family-centered homeschooling education with a greater homeschooling group creates compassion, and children become passionate about changing the world for the better because they experience the communities around them. Four walls do not restrict them; instead, life is their classroom.

The investment of researching and implementing a homeschool education for my adult children has been priceless because it has made them responsible individuals and independent adults. I am raising the bar on self-education and self-development for my daughter. Homeschooling creates inner motivation, which leads children to self-improvement to a whole new level. My daughter actively seeks inspiration and zeal, and each day I devote time to learning new ways to ignite her passions and propel her toward success.

Remember, homeschooling can be very affordable, and the internet is a cornucopia of resources and allows supervised learning with every possible medium! When you research legitimate educational audio, videos, eBooks, etc., you can provide an excellent resource for online education. The life skills courses, academic classes, art lessons, etc., are available at the click of a mouse. Children can find anything they want to learn about, taught by some of the best experts on the planet! Self-development is a priority for any homeschooling plan. Mastering new skills is essential, and keeping interests ignited by focusing on passions and incorporating them into a child's daily schedule is important. The gifts of homeschooling are reserving time each day to learn new information, focus on developing new talents, and discover new challenges to expand the child's intellectual limits. These moments create an unbreakable bond between parent and child. When homeschooling is done correctly, it strengthens skills in stress reduction and joyful living. Finding new ways to enable educational freedom by molding a learning style best suited for children to grow is a blessing.

If I can do it successfully, so can you! Take the Maverick Homeschool Methods and create the ideal academic learning your child deserves. Most importantly, take charge of your child's education! If you believe in choice and educational freedom, you have everything you need in this book to create a worthwhile academic curriculum developed with your child's individual needs in mind and facilitated by you.

The beauty of homeschooling is you are not at the mercy of a predefined timeline; homeschooling gives your child time to master the subjects at their pace to allow foundational learning to flourish. It focuses on the academic journey as an adventure instead of completing a checklist of one daunting task after another. You get to focus and highlight their strengths, and homeschooling leaves you precious time to enjoy the essential milestones they accomplish, and you get to experience their excitement of learning.

Don't let the myths of homeschooling hold you back; you got this!

How to Make Homeschooling a Breeze

To implement a successful learning environment in your home, you need to make the best use of the resources at your disposal.

Fortunately, everything is available on the web, so you have access to thousands of resources to help you.

Unfortunately, everything is available on the web, so you must choose the right ones among the thousands of resources available to you.

Once you find these resources, you also need to determine:

- Which ones are good – Specifically which ones are a good fit for your child's particular needs?
- Which ones are a waste of time and money – Since home-schooling is not rigidly regimented, some unscrupulous companies provide services that aren't always worth the money you spend on them.
- Which resources are available locally – Do you have to buy all the tools you need to educate your children? Or can you barter with other parents and get the tools you need?
- How do you put all these resources together, so they make a coherent plan for your child?

You may need someone to put this all together for you.

Resources to Get You Started

When I work with clients, the first thing I do is show parents the resources useful for them to begin homeschooling. I teach parents the steps to locate homeschooling neighborhood support communities near their home and online.

Here are some important homeschooling resources:

- **Local museums and venues for outings.** These are great ways to help children experience what they learn. You can build an entire year's science curriculum by visiting a science museum multiple times per year.

- **Homeschool co-ops.** These are groups of homeschooling families that meet up regularly to work on common goals together. These can vary from academic, social gatherings, time for the arts, activities or crafts, service work or projects. A co-op is led by parents, and they may contribute a fee or start fundraisers to pay all or some of the enrichment teachers and activity leaders. There may be as few as three families or as many as several hundred children participating in a neighborhood homeschool co-op.

In these communities, you can find resources to help you from a material and curriculum point of view; support in difficult situations; and even parents share teaching duties. These communities can coalesce around homeschooling, world schooling, unschooling, or any other type of alternative learning approach.

- **Prebuilt programs.** These are programs that you can use to create a schedule and a plan that suits your child and you. These programs can provide high school level courses (like math, for example) and provide many other resources such as:
  o Online classrooms
  o Tutors (ones that fit well with your child and you)
  o Live classes
  o Monitoring of classes (so you can make sure that the student is attending class as expected)

- **Online classes**:
  o **Outschool.com** provides interactive online classes for kids aged 3-18.
  o **Time4learning.com** provides a high-quality online learning curriculum for students as well as tools for parents.
  o **Powerhomeschool.org** is a homeschooling program that offers parents the convenience of accessing resources at their own pace. It gives them plenty of choice when it comes to picking courses (grades PreK-12) and allows their children to learn at an individual rate.

There are thousands of these types of resources available.

The challenge is to find the best one for you.

If this seems like a lot, it is, but don't worry. There are educational consultants and managers to help families navigate these choices.

Get Help Putting It All Together

After many years of seeing families suffering through the same types of problems that I had with my children and what I experienced when I was a teacher, I knew I had to help guide parents of children who have different learning styles to take charge of their child's education and direct the best learning avenue that suits their families. Whether it is homeschooling through a district charter school, a PSA, PSS, private school, or public school, know your rights as parents and the choices you have.

It's the reason I wrote this book. I couldn't stand by and watch parents go through the same challenges I had, simply because they didn't know where to start with homeschooling.

The Time Challenge

If you have a full-time job, it may not leave you enough time to take care of all the preparation needed for a great learning environment. This preparation includes planning activities, building a curriculum, and conducting the learning sessions. Even if you are working at home, it's not easy to carve time away from your job to manage a classroom.

If you want to be a homeschooling parent, you also need to understand the various methods that can help your child learn.

If you don't have the time to do all of this on your own, the best way to get fast results is to hire outside help in the form of an educational homeschool consultant.

An educational homeschool consultant acts as a buffer between you and the education system. They help you take charge of your child's education. They make sure that all the services your child needs are provided to them.

Working with an Educational Homeschool Consultant

An educational homeschool consultant is an expert in alternative and traditional education. A talented educational homeschool consultant understands local state education homeschool laws, and they can help build a lawful and beneficial personalized educational plan for children with invisible learning disabilities, 2e kids, gifted kids, and traditional learners.

Educational homeschool consultants free you from the difficult task of creating the learning approach, and let you focus on strategy instead. They have a wealth of information at their disposal, and they share that information with you. They provide you with choices while explaining the benefits and the drawbacks of each option. Then, you have all the information to decide which approach you want to use with your child.

Your educational homeschool consultant then makes sure that your child's educational plan is executed according to your wishes.

Courses and Resources I Provide for Families

My goal is to give parents the correct information to guide families in the right direction, so homeschooling is easy and efficient. I teach parents how to significantly save time which relieves stress, allowing parents to create the best-individualized learning path available for their child.

I will help you navigate and implement homeschooling in your life by:

- Showing you all the various types of curricula you can use: Montessori, Waldorf, unschooling, and many more
- Guiding you through the local laws that you must respect
- Helping you find the best resources based on your child's learning style
- Teaching you how to prepare your learning space in your home
- Finding the best methods and curriculum for your special needs child with invisible learning differences
- Explaining preparation needed to homeschool a high school student efficiently
- Discussing methods of successful socialization while home-schooling

There is a lot to learn, and you can learn it.

My courses guide you with my experience with homeschooling, and you learn how to design curricula for all types of learners to kickstart your homeschooling lifestyle.

Would you like to start your homeschooling experience stress-free?

I want that for you, and here is how I can help you.

I have 22 years combined experience in education as an academic theater director, reading resource specialist, lead classroom Montessori teacher for ages 6-9, educational homeschool consultant, IEP coach and family advocate, and homeschooling parent.

I have the answers your family is seeking to find a unique, specialized program for your child and your family learning experiences.

The Resenbeck Maverick Homeschool Methods provide:

- **Homeschooling courses for parents looking for alternatives to traditional instruction and who have chosen to homeschool their child successfully.**

  The way your district or school dispenses education is not the only way. You will discover teaching methods that are perfectly suited to your child.

- **I show parents where to find local homeschooling laws in their state.**

  It will help you avoid issues with the district and let you know what you are allowed to do in your state to improve your child's learning.

- **Information will be provided about private homeschooling and why finding co-op programs in your community is important.**

It saves you time you can use to take care of your family or meet your job obligations.

- **I give you directions on how to file your local home-school paperwork.**

Once again, this saves you time and stress because you will always know that you have done everything right.

- **I show parents where to find private home-school grants.**

The grants help reduce your financial burden.

- **I show you the steps you take to create a yearly academic program based on the individual needs, talents, and passions of the 'whole child'.**

Your child doesn't get a cookie-cutter education but a specifically tailored program for them, guaranteeing better results than traditional schooling.

- **I give the blueprints on how to homeschool through charter schools and receive academic funds (in some states) from the local school district.**

Each state has its own rules and programs. I inform and help you understand which options are better for your specific situation.

- **As an IEP parent coach and family advocate, I provide professional courses showing parents who have children with invisible learning differences such as dyslexia, dyspraxia, dysgraphia, dyscalculia, ADHD, Asperger's, and Autism spectrum, and more, to homeschool successfully.**

  You don't have to learn everything yourself. You get the benefit of the more than 22 years I spent successfully guiding and helping kids with invisible learning differences.

- **I show families how to navigate the special education process and homeschooling.**

  Your child will not be bouncing around between services that end up not helping them.

- **In my role as IEP Coach, I provide IEP records review, coaching packages, IEP meeting attendance, parent-teacher workshops, and speaking events.**

  The IEP process is complicated and difficult to navigate. I relieve you of that stress and make sure your child gets all the services they are entitled to.

- **I advocate for families of children with invisible learning differences. It doesn't matter if the child is homeschooled, attends private school, or goes to their local public school. I can help ensure their IEP and other accommodations and modifications are being met and following federal laws.**

I show you how to fight the tough battles with the powers that be, so you can get peace of mind about your child's education.

My educational homeschool courses provide families the opportunity to shape unique learning experiences like world schooling, unschooling, and other unconventional ways to teach and school their children.

I guide parents about the different homeschooling educational pedagogies, methods, philosophies, and styles.

It can be a scary and daunting task to navigate your child's education, their exceptional gifts, and IEP services, but never feel helpless.

I show you how to take charge of your child's education, so you can launch the best learning approach for your kids. You will be able to step outside the box and provide your child with the best individualized educational experience you can give them to succeed into adulthood.

As your child's facilitator of learning, using the techniques I provide hands you the tools to develop a personalized academic homeschool plan to reach all levels of learning success because you know your child's learning needs best.

So, stop doubting yourself, stop sitting on the fence, and don't listen to the myths! Take charge of your child's education. Remember, you can develop a tailored program that works for your whole family. You can do this!

About the Author

Mary Resenbeck is an unlikely educator. She became a teacher in 2000 after watching her dyslexic son struggle in a traditional school environment. Determined to help her son, and later her daughter, she became a teacher so she could be at the same school as her children. During her time in the classroom Mary discovered a unique approach to engaging kids across the spectrum from those with "Invisible Learning Differences", to traditional learners, gifted students, and twice-exceptional kids (because they are 2e), like her children. She developed The Resenbeck's Maverick Homeschool Methods and coaches homeschooling families to help them implement the different techniques to make homeschooling efficient, fun, and stress-free.